. . . .

THE MIRACLE OF MAVERICK

An Inspiring True Story to Energize your Heart and Make You Believe in Miracles!

Kelli Davis

Thank you for purchasing and sharing this book.
All proceeds benefit Children's Miracle Network Hospitals
to help other amazing children like Maverick
at children's hospitals across North America.

. . . .

To Maverick:

I love you, buddy! Thank you for showing me how to be brave, how to make the most of each day, and how to love in a bigger, better way!

To Kevin:

You're the man! This Miracle would have never happened without you! I will forever be grateful for your BIG heart and your love for Maverick!

To Big Papi:

Thank you for being the hero who delivered for Maverick!

**This book is dedicated
to every kid in a children's hospital**
and to each beautiful and inspiring young soul
who has touched my heart.

Thank you
Briggs Berry, Christopher Armstrong and Jacob Mockbee
for showing me how to live a life with courage, faith, love and
fearlessness. The light you brought to this world will forever
illuminate my heart.

Always remembered, never forgotten!

Contents

Preface

The positive impact of each miracle child on their family and their community is significant. We are so grateful for all the people who have given to Children's Miracle Network Hospitals to help create miracles and healing for so many families across North America. It is a privilege and honor to be associated with amazing kids like Maverick. I hope his bravery will touch your heart in a meaningful way, like it has mine. **Maverick and his story represents the millions of children who every year face similar health challenges.**

John Lauck
President and CEO - Children's Miracle Network Hospitals

For 35 years I've had the honor of working with Children's Miracle Network Hospitals and I have met hundreds of kids who have faced incredible challenges. In playing professional football I've been hit hard and have faced some big challenges, yet when learning about the incredible resilience and determination of these miracle kids, my challenges on the field seem relatively small compared to those faced by these real champions with miracle hearts of gold. These kids are at a level beyond anything I've witnessed in my experience in professional sports. Their champion stories of miracles, healing, and getting up when the going is tough are a remarkable inspiration to me. Maverick is one of those kids who just keeps getting up!

Steve Young
NFL Hall of Fame Quarterback

Introduction

Don't wait for a miracle. Be the Miracle!

Do you remember what you were doing on Monday, January 29, 1996? I do! It was my first day of work at Children's Miracle Network Hospitals in Salt Lake City. I had just left my lifelong dream job with the National Football League working for the Denver Broncos, and I wasn't quite sure this nonprofit company, which I had never heard of, was going to be the best fit for me. I was a sports fanatic and I was leaving professional sports behind to go to a small, older office in Holladay, Utah. Looking back, 23 years later, I had no idea how this job would change my life, shape my life, and most importantly make me "Believe in Miracles."

Children's Miracle Network Hospitals is an amazing foundation which raises funds and awareness for 170 children's hospitals across North America, treats 10 million kids each year, and makes sure all the money stays local. Sadly, my 23-year-old mind wasn't grasping the magnitude of the opportunity I was being given. I was concerned that I was leaving my dream job and wondering if I could find something I would ever love as much.

But hindsight is an amazing perspective.

I've learned that life doesn't always go as planned—it is much often better. These amazing kids I've met didn't plan on having such difficult challenges and setbacks. But life happens and in every challenge there is a gift and opportunity.

I thought I would be married and have four children, but that didn't happen for me. Instead, I am still single and have more than 100 kids I like to call my own.

2

These amazing children and their families are my family. They are angels walking on earth, leaving imprints on my heart, and teaching me and the rest of us how to truly live.

I'm sure as you read this book about one of these kids, sweet Maverick, you may think of a single child, or many children, whose story needs to be told so it can impact the world the way it has impacted your life.

Their lives, their struggles, their triumphs, their tears, their joys are not just for me, you, and their families to know about. They are here to change us, to help us, to encourage us, to inspire us, to teach us, to ground us, to humble us, to shape us, to make us "Believe in Miracles."

So my question for you is... Do you believe in miracles?

Whether you believe in yourself, humanity, nature, physics, some unseen connection, a higher power, God or some variation of joyful miracles, the purpose of this book is to help you believe in and most importantly help create miracles in the lives around you, especially those miracle kids at your local children's hospital.

You never know when you, a neighbor, friend or family member might need a children's hospital, and I can't think of anything more rewarding than to know you are helping a sick child get better.

When you finish reading, my hope is that you will feel as though you know Maverick, and that his story will make a positive difference in your life. Perhaps his story might forever impact the way you embrace your life, the way you choose to live each day, the way you show up for yourself and others.

So enjoy the read, but please do me a favor! Find your own Maverick within.

Here are three ideas for your consideration when you are finished reading:

1) Make sure you tell just one person about Maverick.
2) Commit to making a miracle happen within the next week for a total stranger, loved one, or frankly anyone on the planet.
3) Give a donation large or small to a children's hospital. Go to www.cmnhospitals.org to donate.

If we all come together to create miracles we will create a ripple effect of miracles that can't be stopped. Thank you!

Kelli Davis

David Ortiz (aka Big Papi) and Maverick Schutte

Chapter One
DO YOU BELIEVE IN MIRACLES? I DO.

"What might be possible?"

Do you believe in miracles? I do.

If you're like most people, you might feel stuck or broken in some way, while experiencing family hardships, serious health issues, or financial troubles. Perhaps you are suffering from a broken heart, broken dreams, or a broken home. You might be struggling with emotional or mental health issues, traumas, addictions, or abuse in your family or neighborhood.

Maybe you're having difficulties at school or at work. Maybe you have no job or no place to call home. Maybe you feel sad, lonely, depressed, or hurt in some way. You might be bullied at school, work, or on social media. You may be feeling insecure, insignificant, or inside out and upside-down. Perhaps you are trying to win and you just can't seem to connect to make it happen. Maybe you feel as though you are chasing a carrot on a stick and still searching for an ever elusive breakthrough, promotion, scholarship, healing, or inner peace.

Problems and challenges are real. They can be serious and difficult. Maybe you are a child in a children's hospital trying to find the strength to get better. Maybe you are a pre-teen dealing with puberty. Maybe you are a teenager trying to make sense of life or win your game. Perhaps as an adult you are struggling in a marriage or with the pace of life. Or maybe you are an aging senior trying to make sense of the loss of control, or searching deep inside yourself to realize what your real contribution was in life —your legacy.

In all their many varieties, seen and unseen, roadblocks, setbacks, and challenges show up in life for everyone. In all their many varieties, seen and unseen, miracles also show up in life for everyone. I believe miracles do indeed show up in our lives more than we might recognize.

Do you believe in miracles? I do.

What are your deepest wishes and what seems to be blocking your path? Might there be someone who could help ease your burden in some way or make your journey a little easier right now? Might there be a new discovery or a new piece of information which could make all the difference in the world? Could a little tiny effort from many people contribute to making a miracle in your world? Children's Miracle Network Hospitals knows that a small amount of change from many people can raise millions and make a huge and positive change in the lives of sick kids across North America. I've personally seen many miracles, and in this book, I'm going to share the Miracle of Maverick.

Do you believe in miracles? I do.

It's okay if right now in this moment, you honestly feel that miracles don't happen. You've been hurt. You've been scared. You've been let down. You've tried and things didn't work out. You gave your best and it wasn't enough. You laid it out on the line and got crushed. You've trusted before, but feel that trusting and vulnerability is for suckers. You want to be courageous, but it is hard to trust and be vulnerable in all this overwhelming uncertainty.

Yes, right now in this moment, it may seem very hard for you to believe in miracles for many reasons. Perhaps you believe miracles actually do happen, but you sincerely believe they only happen to other people, right? Maybe you feel that somehow you have been left out. Perhaps you say to yourself, "Okay, miracles may happen to other people, but they don't happen to me." Maybe you feel you're the exception to the rule. I invite you to break that rule of conformity and other rules that say it can't be done—and honestly allow a miracle in your life. I invite you to challenge the assumption that a real miracle somehow can't happen to you. I believe that not only can a miracle indeed happen to you, I believe you can also help create a miracle in someone else's life.

I invite you to be open to the possibility that a miracle might be right around the corner for you. What might it be like to experience a powerful miracle in your life? What might it be like to know with confident certainty that such a thing, a real miracle, is indeed possible?

A miracle might be on delivery right now and will arrive sooner than you think. Perhaps an unexpected phone call? Perhaps a kind and encouraging word from a stranger or friend? Perhaps an amazing job opportunity? What might be possible? What might that positive new reality feel like for you?

8

Maybe you are about to experience a turbo boost of healing. Maybe you are a phone call away from the best news of your life. Maybe you are one step away from a loving text that authentically changes the direction of your life in a lasting and significant way. Maybe you are one simple moment away from winning your game.

Perhaps your miracle might come through a flash of inspiration. Maybe your miracle will show up as money to pay your bills or fund your big dream goal. Maybe your miracle will take place with you on the giving side of a donation and contribution of your time and resources. Maybe your miracle will show up as a successful surgery or medical procedure. Perhaps your miracle is a successful study session or a better grade on your test. Maybe your miracle could be a smile or a boost of courage and confidence to see the joy in life again. Maybe today you will find someone who shows up with empathy and heartfelt connection to make your problems and challenges seem solvable and doable.

Do you believe in miracles? I do.

I invite you to consider the idea that a miracle is ready to come into your life in a very real and powerful way. For just a moment, as you read this book and hear this amazing story of my dear friend Maverick. I invite you to pause your judgement, self-doubts, negative self-talk, and internal criticism. You can certainly come back to visit those later. But just for a moment, just for right now, I invite you to be open to the idea that a miracle is waiting to come into your life. Yes—a real MIRACLE IN YOUR LIFE, customized perfectly for you. I am hopeful that in reading this inspiring true story, you will re-awaken to the realization that miracles are REAL and indeed possible!

You have a choice, you always have a choice. You can choose to be open to the idea of miracles showing up in your life in many real and practical ways, or you can choose to close your mind to the possibility of allowing miracles to show up in your world. Decide for yourself, but as for me, I choose miracles.

Do you believe in miracles? I do.

2

Chapter Two
THE MIRACLE OF MAVERICK

*"We become miracle makers when we
choose to allow and participate in
miracles."*

In my wildest dreams I couldn't make this story up! But it actually happened! I continually remind myself this wasn't a dream. It was real! I was there! I experienced it!

In some small way I helped facilitate the story, but it wasn't about me. It was about a higher purpose involving miracles for six-year-old Maverick Schutte and many other people, including me.

Whatever your perception of "miracles" may be, I've learned there is definitely a harmonious goodness orchestrated purposefully to create amazing, miraculous occurrences. I believe when we show up with courage and love, miracles happen. We might call it God, Source, Nature, Spirit, Soul Connection, A Higher Power, Our Best from Within, or something else. I believe this greater good, this unseen beautiful magic, often depends on our choosing to involve our own willing hands and hearts.

We become miracle makers when we
choose to allow and participate in

miracles. We can seek for, pray for, and look for opportunities to assist. We can be bold and courageous in action. Afterwards, we often smile with deep gratitude and joy, again and again, reflecting on that powerful miracle that transformed lives in positive ways--and somehow still continues to do so long after the event.

I had no idea how much my life would change by meeting Maverick Schutte! In June 2014, I was at the JW Marriott in Washington, DC on a business trip for Children's Miracle Network Hospitals, a nonprofit organization that raises funds for 170 children's hospitals across North America. I've been blessed to work for the organization for 18 years.

It was a beautiful summer day, and I was stationed at the check-in table at the entry of the hotel. My team and I were greeting children who had just flown in for our champions' event, a special occasion for which 50 miracle kids, one from each state, had been hand selected and invited to serve as ambassadors for the 10 million children we treat each year at our hospitals. Our responsibility was to welcome our guests, ask a few questions, provide direction, and help each champion child and parents with any special needs for the event.

As fate would have it, our Wyoming champion, Maverick, and his Mom, Marti, happened to come to my check-in line, and I bonded with this cute kid instantly!

It was a miracle from the start. When checking in, each champion child confirmed the correct information for their birthday. This information was necessary for our special visit to the White House to meet with the First Lady, Michelle Obama. When I learned that Maverick and I were both from Wyoming and shared the same June birthday, we were both amazed! I will never forget Maverick's response when I told him the news.

"Oh my gosh, I can't believe we have the same birthday!" His voice, his smile, his sincerity, his pure joy, his energy was palpable. You could feel his infectious spirit and energy for life. There was something special about this kid that just made you want to be around him. Even in that simple first encounter, I felt an undeniable connection with this remarkable child. Little did I know that we had just embarked on a friendship that would last a lifetime.

What makes Maverick so special?

Some might say it's his larger-than-life personality, but Maverick's medical challenges since birth, including five open heart surgeries, make Maverick a super special kid, one who is able to experience pain while choosing to have a big smile on his face.

Maverick is a superhero and has superhuman powers! Even though he is small in stature, he defines what it means to be a hero by his enormous courage! He doesn't let 40 plus surgeries stop him from smiling, making people laugh, or soaking up the most of every moment.

One reason I especially love Maverick is the joy and courage he displays again and again, no matter what the circumstance or challenge. To me, that is a HUGE miracle! Meeting each challenge, in each moment, time-after-time, year-after-year, has earned Maverick an advanced degree in resilience and perseverance. How does such a young kid like Maverick show up with such joy and courage? He chooses it!

Maverick has a list of diagnoses hard to fathom. It is difficult to believe someone can go through all of that and still be alive. Most people would call that a medical miracle. Another miracle is that somehow, despite all of his medical issues, or perhaps because of them, Maverick chooses to be a very happy little guy with an energizing positive attitude!

The minute Maverick was born he began the fight of his life. Maverick was born with a heart defect known as Tetralogy of Fallot, a chronic lung disease, a small airway passage which makes breathing difficult, a sideways curvature of the spine, a kidney disorder, an infection in his heart, an enlarged liver, low blood sugar, a heart rhythm disorder, and a bone disease which causes weak and brittle bones and many other medical complications.

I often wonder what it would be like to be in Maverick's shoes and live with his long list of health challenges. What would it feel like to have a sick heart? How would it feel to spend so much time in the hospital? What goes through a six- year-old's mind when he meets with doctor after doctor? Maybe a good place to start for a little perspective and context is hearing it first-hand from Maverick's mom, Marti.

3

Chapter Three
HEAVEN IS REAL!

"We won't stop working until our mission is complete"

Marti's perspective: Even though there were times that I felt like everything was against us, Maverick has always found his way through.

Maverick has had two cardiac arrests in his life.

One was at home with a tracheostomy plug. His four-year-old sister helped bag him while I did chest compressions until his aunt arrived to assist me; and 911 arrived to take over.

The second was the worst day of my life! Maverick was in the ICU with pneumonia. For days he had been telling the staff and me he was going to die. I wasn't sure what he meant by this. I was trying to reassure him he would be fine but he DID NOT want me to leave his side. After sneaking out for a quick restroom break I returned to find Maverick looking me dead in the eyes and telling me again he was

15

going to die. Suddenly the machines went off and just like that, my baby was gone. Maverick's potassium had skyrocketed to a 10. The best team, in my eyes, did everything they could do, yet it seemed like hours before they miraculously were able to save Maverick. I was on the floor screaming, surrounded by doctors and nurses who had heard the code and knew it was Maverick. They had come rushing to be by my side. Even his main pulmonologist was called and returned to the hospital.

The most chilling part of this experience is that Maverick had a "passing over." He remembers God doing chest compressions, and the angels who held his hand. He will tell you all of this, where he was, and where all the staff members were standing.

Heaven is for real!

I call Maverick my Benjamin Button. He is wise beyond his years but the size of a three-year-old. He doesn't miss a beat and he doesn't forget a thing. He has a BIG voice. When Maverick was very young I was faced with the difficult decision of placing a tracheostomy. It is a high-risk procedure to have a tube place placed in the windpipe. Maverick learned to walk and talk with the tracheostomy and ventilator in place. It seemed as if nothing could or would hold Maverick down no matter what new challenge he faced. Maverick never said no and never gave up. When Maverick was six-years-old he was able to get the tracheostomy removed.

Maverick may be behind academically, but he is so smart. He is the funniest kid I know. Recently we were asked who his writer was and told that he should have his own sitcom. He loves superheroes and baseball.

Maverick will face challenges every day, but we still

have Maverick. We celebrate birthdays! We get to be the face for the cause of Children's Miracle Network Hospitals. We won't stop working until our mission is complete. We have a mission, and that mission is #maverickstrong.

4

Chapter Four
ASK FOR MIRACLES

"...it's about the miracles you can create in someone's life"

Ask for Miracles. Now that you have a little background and context, let's flashback to Washington, DC to my first meeting with Maverick. While sharing time together with these 50 miracle kids for a few days, I observed and learned something unique and powerful about these champions. All of them, and especially Maverick, show up with elevated positive emotions, and they ask for miracles in the everyday, moment by moment.

Let me share a fun example. As part of our special Children's Miracle Network Hospitals event, we received the opportunity to meet Miss America, Kira Kazantzev, who served as the National Goodwill Ambassador for the organization. She is beautiful, and I imagine many guys across the country would love to go on a date with such a smart, attractive, talented, and inspiring woman. Most guys might shy away from asking her out, or perhaps think they don't even have a chance. Not these miracle kids. They are fearless!

I was awestruck, amazed, and filled with joy watching Maverick and his cute friend Nolan, our adorable champion from Nebraska, ask Kira if they could have her phone number.

Imagine the cutest, most innocent little voices saying, "Miss America, can we please have your phone number?" These champions create miracles every day. Watching these two that day was priceless.

Heart of Gold. When you are in Maverick's presence you need a notepad because everything he says is quotable. He has the power to command a room, a sense of humor that makes everyone instantly fall in love with him, and most importantly, a heart of gold.

At such a young age, he realizes that those around him have problems, too. In fact, when I asked him what makes him a champion, he says it's because he collected toys and donated them to the kids at Children's Hospital Colorado.

Big 6th Birthday. Because of all Maverick's endearing traits, our shared birthday, and our mutual connection to Wyoming, I had a huge desire to do something special for him for his sixth birthday.

Knowing that Maverick loves the TV show Phineas and Ferb, I spent quite a bit of time tracking down Vincent Martella, the man who is the voice of Phineas. Thankfully, I was finally able to contact Vincent and get him to call Maverick on his birthday.

I can't explain the joy that happens when you make dreams come true for those around you. There is no better feeling, especially for a sick child who doesn't know his future. Thanks to Maverick's mom, who videotaped the call, I got to watch the big smile on Maverick's face while he sat in disbelief and talked to his favorite TV character, Phineas.

I could have decided it was too difficult to track down Phineas. I could have given up when I experienced setbacks, delays, and challenges, but when you are thinking about others instead of being focused on yourself, there is no obstacle that can prevent you from making miracles happen for kids who deserve it most. To me it's not about how much time it will require or how hard it might be. Rather, it's about what kind of miracle you can create in someone's life.

We have such power to be a miracle in the lives of those around us. A simple wave, a smile, a kind word, a wink, a gesture, letting someone in line, sending a simple thank-you card, making dinner, giving someone a ride, saying you're sorry, offering forgiveness—these are such simple things, but these simple things can make this world a great place to live!

5

Chapter Five
IT WAS A MIRACLE

"...the man who hits the home runs."

Boston Red Sox. Speaking of miracles, this next story was made possible by Maverick's mom, Marti, because she married Mike Linanne, a guy from back east who loves the Boston Red Sox! When Mike started dating Marti, watching the Red Sox was a way for the family to bond, and of course, Maverick fell in love with the Boston Red Sox, too!

When Marti and Mike got married they even wore Red Sox Jerseys. After watching many games, Maverick was enthralled and absolutely in love with David Ortiz (aka Big Papi) because, in Maverick's words, "he is the man who hits the home runs." If you follow baseball at all, you know that Big Papi is one of the best home-run hitters to ever play the game and also one of nicest players on the planet. He is a legend with a huge heart for kids and giving back.

Knowing that Maverick loved the Red Sox, I made the most of the opportunity I had to be with two of the best Red Sox players and World Series champions, Josh Beckett and Kevin Millar. We were in Hawaii in early February 2016 for the 19th Annual Ace Hardware Golf Shootout, which benefits Children's Miracle Network Hospitals.

During the event, I reached out to Maverick to send me a special video I could show Kevin and Josh, which he did without hesitation! It started with Maverick in a Red Sox shirt holding up a Big Papi Lego and saying, "Hi Josh, and Kevin, my name is Maverick, M-A-V-E-R-I-C-K, my favorite people in the Red Sox is Big Papi, and any place I want to go is Fenway Park, and you are "wicked cool."

After I got the message I told Marti I would send the video to Kevin. She wrote back, "I can't even express what diehard Red Sox fans we are. We even had to switch cable companies just so we could get MLB extra innings and NESN."

After sending the video, I got a video back from Josh and Kevin for Maverick which said, "You are the best, you are the champion. I'm going to tell Big Papi all about you and I'm going to tell him that Big Maverick is a fan. And Papi is your biggest fan, and I'm going to try to get him to tell you hello when I see him at Spring Training Camp."

Then Sweet Maverick sent a video back to them saying, "Are you sure you are going to tell Big Papi all about me?" You gotta love this kid!

Big Papi. So my dream was to get Big Papi to give

Maverick a shout out. I let a few months go by, and since Maverick wasn't doing very well, I reached out to Kevin Millar to see if he could get in touch with Big Papi. Kevin told me Big Papi had changed his number, and he didn't have his current information. I didn't think about this again until April 29th when I saw an Instagram post of Kevin with his sweet boys, Kash and Kanyon, at Fenway Park with Big Papi.

I immediately texted Kevin and said, "Any chance Big Papi could tell Mavs hi on your phone?"

Kev texted back 30 minutes later, "Ah-h-h-h-h-h yes, let me do that, send me a picture of Mav." I quickly sent a picture and two hours and 15 minutes later I had a video from Big Papi and Kevin Millar saying:

David Ortiz: "Hey, little Maverick, what's happening buddy, how you doin'? I hope you're doin' great, stay positive. Big Papi right here with my boy Kevin. We love you! So remember that, WE love you!

Kevin: "Ok! Cowboy up, we're always on your side, always!"

David: "Stay positive, keep the faith. All right, you take care, buddy, and *I'm going to hit a homerun for you tonight!*"

Kevin: "He's hitting a homerun for you Maverick, Bye!"

On the brink of a Miracle. I immediately

sent the video to Maverick, and his mom posted on Facebook, "Maverick is freaking out right now. This video made his day. He jumped on top of me saying 'this is the best day of my life.' Mom cried. His hero sent him a video."

I was SO happy that Maverick got a video from his hero that I didn't even think about watching the game. The likelihood of Big Papi hitting a homerun for Maverick wasn't something I thought would happen. Who hits a home run just because they promise one? The odds of getting a hit, let alone a home run aren't very good, even if you're one of the greatest players in Major League Baseball.

That evening, while I was in my bedroom cleaning and surfing the TV stations, I was divinely guided to the promised home run game just in time to watch big Papi strike out.

Every time Papi stepped up to bat, I was down on my knees praying for a miracle because I knew what it would mean to Maverick if his hero hit a home run just for him.

So envision this! It's the bottom of the 8th inning at Fenway Park, and the Boston Red Sox are playing their biggest rival, the New York Yankees!

Big Papi steps up to bat. He's 0-3 that night against one of the best relief pitchers in the game, someone he's never had a hit off of in his entire career.

Big Papi holds his bat up and stands ready at the plate. And then he does it!!! He hits a two-run, home run to put the Red Sox up and win the game 4-2.

I freaked out when Big Papi hit the home run!! I was jumping up and down screaming and crying! I don't remember wanting anything so badly.

It was a miracle! In that moment I was so grateful because I knew God answered prayers. I already knew that he did, but it was confirmed again, and all I could say was "thank you, thank you, thank you!"

Thankfully, Marti was videoing the game when Big Papi hit the home run. Maverick yells "Yes!! He hit that one just for me?" and Marti responded, "Yes, Baby, he hit that just for you!"

If you know Maverick, then you know that gratitude is on his mind, and I immediately got a video from him saying "Big Papi, you never let me down, and you are the best player ever in the Red Sox GAME and I'm trying the hardest to get out there to Fenway Park and meet you. Bye. Great homer—we saw it!"

At that moment I realized I had just witnessed a miracle and the world needed to know this story. I started texting my boss and other team members telling them about this crazy miracle. I mean you don't just hit a home run every day in Major League Baseball! It's very hard to do, especially when you are having a rough night at bat and on top of that you make a promise to a sick kid.

Thankfully, my boss was able to string together videos from Maverick, Big Papi, and Kevin to create a cool story. Children's Miracle Network Hospitals posted this video on our social media, as did Kevin and Big Papi. The next morning when I woke up the story had gone viral. Matt Younis with Channel 5 in Boston reached out first to talk to Marti, and that was the beginning of media interviews for Maverick and Marti with ABC World News Tonight, Fox and Friends, ESPN, and more. The story was everywhere!

It was a thrill to see ABC World News tonight do a feature on Maverick. Marti said, "We are just a small-town family, fighting for Mavs' life, and he loves his Red Sox. This is so crazy!! We knew what that home run meant, but now the world knows and it's unbelievable. I went to bed and woke in the morning to find our little boy trending all over social media. You ask him how he feels, and he says, 'Cool, I knew he wouldn't let me down.'"

For several days there was a media firestorm; everybody wanted to talk about the Miracle at the Ballpark, especially to Maverick and his family who had to keep rewatching the story to believe it.

The day before this miracle happened Marti posted on Facebook, "Our family really needs a miracle!" Who would have thought the miracle would come in less than 24 hours in the coolest way possible?

In an interview the following day with NESN, Big Papi commented about the home run. "It was very touching, and

I started thinking about it when I got home. I was really like, I can't believe this really happened. It is what it is. His parents haven't seen him that happy, I am a huge believer in God, and God makes special things happen."

Big Papi has made three promises to sick kids and he is batting a 1,000; he is 3-for-3. Now that is a MIRACLE!

6

Chapter Six
COULD IT GET ANY BETTER?

"When you think of someone else before yourself, you can make little and BIG miracles happen."

Could It Get Any Better? Now if the story ended here it would be an amazing story, but God had such big plans for Maverick and his family. At 11:22 a.m. on April 30th I received a text message from Kevin saying "I need to fly Maverick to Boston on May 11th. I will talk to my buddy, Uncle Loddie, who has the plane, and maybe we can get this to happen if he's healthy enough."

I immediately went to Marti to tell her the exciting news. It was going to be a challenge because Maverick was still pretty sick and needed to get clearance from his pulmonologist and cardiologist to be able to travel. Thankfully, another miracle happened, and Maverick received clearance. I let Kevin know and he began to work his magic.

For those of you who don't know, Kevin Millar is a former professional baseball first baseman who played in Major League Baseball (MLB) and is a current analyst for MLB Network and hosts *Intentional Talk*. He played in MLB for the Florida Marlins, Boston Red Sox, Baltimore Orioles, and Toronto Blue Jays from 1998 through 2009. He won the World Series with the Boston Red Sox in 2004. He also is a husband, and father to four amazing kids.

By May 8th Kevin had secured the private plane, and we worked to coordinate the details to make sure the plane could handle all of Maverick's medical needs. While Kevin was finding the plane, he was also doing his show, *Intentional Talk*, on the MLB Network, and coaching his kids' baseball games. Kevin was beyond busy, but he prioritized his time and chose to make this happen for his buddy Maverick.

It was nearly impossible to pull off this miracle, but Kevin did it because he loved Maverick. He was determined to make Maverick's dream come true, to meet Big Papi. Without Kevin Millar's big heart this miracle would never have happened.

Wanting the world to know Maverick's story, Kevin arranged for the MLB Network to fly with us on the private plane from Cheyenne to Boston. On May 10th I flew from Salt Lake City to Denver and arrived at Mavs' house around 1:00 p.m. It was so amazing to reunite with this little guy after nearly two years! Getting a hug from Maverick was the best thing ever!

At 2:00 p.m. MLB Network came to the house and taped for two hours. We learned more about Maverick's health challenges, his love for the Red Sox, and how deeply important this miracle was to his family.

Onward to Boston. The next morning we were
up bright and early and departed at 10:00 a.m. to Boston for what we would soon find out was the trip of a lifetime. When

we landed, a vehicle picked us up and drove us to the Marriott Hotel, which was donated by Children's Miracle Network Hospital's amazing corporate partner, the Marriott Vacation Club. Maverick stayed on the top floor. The hotel had given him an amazing gift basket filled with all kinds of goodies including Red Sox sunglasses and a baseball.

The next morning Kevin came to the hotel, and it was magical to watch Maverick and Kevin meet face-to-face for the first time. They bonded instantly and were quickly playing catch in the lobby, with Maverick hitting the ball with his Batman shoe and claiming it was a home run over the Green Monster. Their instant chemistry was obvious— Maverick and Kevin loved each other.

Later that day we arrived at Fenway Park in big anticipation of Maverick meeting his hero. Kevin gave Maverick a personal tour of Fenway Park, while toting around his oxygen tank. Kevin took Maverick inside the

Green Monster, where he and his sister, Taylor, were able to leave their signatures on the wall.

After touring the field, Kevin took Maverick inside to the batting cages, the place designated for Maverick to meet his hero! We all knew a surprise for Maverick was going to be happening very soon and we were all anticipating the BIG moment.

7

Chapter Seven
MEETING HIS HERO

Big Papi! I will never forget the moment Maverick met his HERO. Big Papi walked in the room and Maverick's face lit up with the biggest brightest smile and light in his eyes. Maverick exclaimed, "Big Papi!!!" The two quickly embraced, and it was incredibly heartwarming to watch this little boy from Cheyenne, Wyoming hug his hero!

Thousands of kids would love to meet Big Papi, but Maverick was right there, being embraced by the man he had looked up to for so long!

Big Papi then gave Maverick a special gift. He gave the home run ball to Maverick. Thankfully, the fan who caught the ball had heard of Maverick's story, and wanted Maverick to have it. Now that is a miracle!

More than Just a Game. It was amazing to watch Maverick and Big Papi together! Maverick told Big Papi he was throwing out the first pitch, so Big Papi practiced with him and said, "Ya, you've got this!" Then Big Papi rolled Maverick's oxygen tank upstairs to the locker room where Maverick met all the players before the game.

With his energizing personality, Maverick interacted with the players and team manager, John Farrell. In his

31

adorable cute voice, Maverick told them, "My favorite players are #1 Big Papi, #2 Kevin Millar, #3 Xander Bogaerts, #4 Brock Holt and #5 Clay Buchholz."

We then went out to the field for batting practice. It was delightful to see the big smile on Maverick's face when Big Papi would catch his ball. It was very touching to watch Maverick give some sick kids who were on the sideline a baseball, but that was just Maverick being Maverick— he is always thinking of others!

Before the game began, we watched a special video on the Red Sox big screen starring Maverick, Kevin, and Big Papi. It was completely miraculous that this experience was happening, all as a result of a few videos sent back and forth.

To kick off the game, Maverick got to throw out the first pitch. He walked out on the field with Kevin and Big Papi and threw the pitch to Big Papi after winding up his arm. I asked Maverick who taught him how to do that, and he simply said, "Nobody did, I just did it on my own."

Thanks to Kevin, we had the most prized seats in the ballpark, right next to the Red Sox dugout. Maverick had great fun high-fiving the players when they would go out to bat or come in from hitting. He would yell the general manager's name, "John Farrell" and then John would high-five him. Maverick also kept yelling Big Papi's name, and Big Papi would come right up to Maverick and high-five him. This simple act of kindness, repeated many times during the middle of a game, solidified to me how much Maverick meant to Big Papi.

I was privileged to have Maverick sit on my lap most of the game, except when he was sitting on Kevin's lap. He kept calling me his girlfriend and he wouldn't let me out of his sight. Maverick was on the big screen many times throughout the night, and several fans behind us were chanting Maverick's name, "Maverick, Maverick!" One of them caught a foul ball from Dustin Pedroia and gave the ball to Maverick. Another miracle!

The night was full of surprises, but the coolest moment came when the game was over and Big Papi gave

Maverick his bat! Big Papi didn't have to do that, but he loved Maverick and wanted to make the day perfect for him. And oh, was it perfect! From meeting with Kevin, to the hug with Big Papi, to the locker room experience, to throwing out the first pitch, to hanging out in the dugout, to being gifted two balls and a bat, to a 13-3 win against the Oakland A's, it truly was an unforgettable night.

I didn't want to leave the ballpark that night. It was magical! I realized that so many things had to transpire for that moment in time to take place. I believe God knew what He was doing every step along the way.

The next morning we had one more surprise because Kevin invited us back to the ballpark to meet two-time World Series Champion pitcher, Roger Clemens, before we flew back to Cheyenne.

It was heartbreaking to watch Maverick say goodbye to Kevin. After their long goodbye hug, Maverick cried for a good 15 minutes in the car and couldn't stop talking about his new, best buddy for life and how he wanted to move to Boston. There was no doubt, Kevin had made a huge impact in Maverick's life!

On the plane ride home the next day, I had to process what had occurred. Maverick's Mom said it best, "We are just nobodies from a small town in Wyoming. I can't believe this is happening to us."

When you ask for miracles, you need to believe that they are possible. Anything is possible when you ask God to bless you. God loves Maverick! He worked miracles through many people to make his dream come true. You might think that Kevin and Big Papi were a big part of the dream, but there were many people involved. Think about all his family, friends, nurses, doctors, and everyone who was responsible at the hospital for giving Maverick the best care possible. There were hundreds of people who made it possible for Maverick to experience that miracle on May 11th and everyone's contribution was vital and significant.

Miracles do happen every day, and you have to know that what YOU do every day matters. When you think of someone else before yourself, you can make little and BIG miracles happen. One act of service can change the world, one person at a time and one good deed at a time. You can choose to boldly move into action. Don't let fear get in the way! Do something today for that one person you've felt prompted to help. That prompting isn't made up—it's real! Whom are you being guided to help? Pray to know what you can do for this person. You will get answers. Can God trust you to act on the answers he gives you?

8

Chapter Eight
HOW CAN YOU CREATE A MIRACLE?

"What role do you play?"

So the question is... Who's the hero for whom? Was Big Papi the hero for Maverick or Maverick the hero for Big Papi? Did the miracle happen because Maverick believed in Big Papi or because Big Papi believed in Maverick? The fan who caught Maverick's ball actually gave it back to the Red Sox, and Big Papi gave the ball to Maverick. Sometimes we catch the ball, but we give it to someone else because they need it more than we do. The ball may give someone more hope, more courage. That piece of leather turned into a miracle, a physical manifestation of the miracle. What role do you play?

Everyone, at some time in his or her life, is a Maverick. Everyone at some time in his or her life is a Big Papi, a Kevin Millar, or a ball-catching fan who then gives a game-winning homerun ball to someone else. We all can participate and share in the joy of miracles. At times in our lives we need a miracle. Other times we help create miracles. Other times we are the miracle. And more often than we realize, our seemingly small actions make beautiful miracles happen in meaningful ways. We are all more connected than we might realize.

All of us already are true heroes. Each one of us already has greatness within, in our own unique ways. We are each miracle makers. Each one of us can break the rules of what seems to be impossible to help create miracles. What is your Maverick moment? What specifically are you going to do right now or this week to participate in a miracle in some way? What miracle can you help create? What small or big miracle do you need? What hope can you share? What life can you inspire or touch today or this week? Who needs you to show up with your best A-Game today?

I invite you to commit right now to do something this week to help make a miracle happen in some way.

Do you believe in miracles? I do. We do. Thank you.

....

To watch the MLB Network story, go to untoldmiracles.org/Maverick. Fair warning you will need Kleenex.

9

Chapter Nine
Testimonials, Thanks, and Pictures

"You may never know what results come of your actions, but if you do nothing, there will be no results." —*Mahatma Gandhi*

"Maverick has changed my life by humbling me daily. He has taught me to never give up. If he doesn't give up when

life gets tough, then why should I? It's hard to understand what this little angel from God goes through. Maverick is a tough, powerful little stud, a warrior, and a leader. His smile, attitude and personality light up this world. My favorite thing about Maverick is his laugh. It's so addictive! The giggle, the laugh, the smile.... everything about him makes me happy! He gives the best hugs ever!!! He's my buddy for life!" - *Kevin Millar*

10

Chapter Ten
BE THE MIRACLE TODAY

Sometimes in life you get up to bat, and you strike out. Sometimes you strike out over and over. And then in life there are those moments when you connect. When you really connect and hit a game-winning home run.

To all those inspiring players in life, like Maverick, Big Papi, and YOU, who keep trying and doing their best, again and again--in all the ups and downs--thank you! Your heroic courage, game-winning mindset, and continued effort makes a positive difference in the world. Your true greatness inspires others more than you know. Do you believe in miracles? I do!

I hope you were inspired by reading Maverick's story! If you want to help more kids like Maverick, please consider going to www.CMNhospitals.org to make a donation and help create a miracle in the life of a sick child today. One dollar, five dollars, ten dollars, it all adds up to help save kids' lives!

Children's Miracle Network Hospitals® raises funds for 170 children's hospitals across North America, which, in turn, use the money where it's needed the most. When a donation is given it stays in the community, helping local kids. Since 1983, Children's Miracle Network Hospitals has raised more than $5 billion, most of it $1 at a time. These donations have gone to support research and training, purchase equipment, and pay for uncompensated care, all in support of the mission to save and improve the lives of as many children as possible.

About Kelli Davis

In 1996 Kelli began working with Children's Miracle Network Hospitals. Ms. Davis is the head of celebrity relations for Children's Miracle Network Hospitals, where she works closely with "A" list celebrities to raise funds and awareness for 10 million sick children each year at 170 children's hospitals across North America.

Kelli hosts the "Untold Miracles" podcast and interviews celebrities to discuss the miracles in their personal and professional life.
www.untoldmiracles.org

To learn more about Kelli go to www.bookkellidavis.com

Special thanks to Dennis Allen MBA for your coaching, editing, and support. You've helped me experience so many "Ah-ha" moments--especially in putting together into words this amazing story. You've helped me stay committed and follow through to completion. You've helped me to eloquently say what's in my heart. You've helped me be my true authentic self. You always encourage and energize me. I love your humble non-ego approach to "envision possibility; unfreeze momentum; and actionize joy!"